Collins

easy learning

Spelling

Ages
6–7

How to use this book

- Find a quiet, comfortable place to work, away from distractions.
- Tackle one topic at a time.
- Help with reading the instructions where necessary and ensure that your child understands what to do.
- Help and encourage your child to check their own answers as they complete each activity.
- Discuss with your child what they have learnt.
- Let your child return to their favourite pages once they have been completed, to talk about the activities.
- Reward your child with plenty of praise and encouragement.

Special features

- Yellow boxes: Introduce a topic and outline the key spelling ideas.

- **D** Suggests when your child can use a dictionary to help with the spelling or understanding of a word.

- Orange shaded boxes: Suggest activities and encourage discussion with your child about what they have learnt.

Spelling a new word

When your child is learning to spell, use the 'Look and say, cover, write, check' method:

- Look at the word and say it aloud.
- Cover it.
- Write it.
- Check it.

Reading a new word

- Break up the word into smaller parts, for example: cupboard = cup + board.
- Pronounce the word exactly as it is written, for example: Wed-nes-day.
- Break the word up into separate phonemes (sounds), for example: sh-ee-p.

Published by Collins
An imprint of HarperCollins*Publishers*
1 London Bridge Street
London SE1 9GF

Browse the complete Collins catalogue at
www.collins.co.uk

© HarperCollins*Publishers* Limited 2011
This edition © HarperCollins*Publishers* 2015

10 9 8 7 6 5 4 3

ISBN 978-0-00-813442-6

The author asserts the moral right to be identified as the author of this work.

The author and publisher are grateful to the copyright holders for permission to use the quoted materials and images.

P4 © wawritto/shutterstock.com
P6 © Evellean/shutterstock.com
P7 © Paganin/shutterstock.com
P8 © SvitalskyBros/Shutterstock.com, © nanami7/Shutterstock.com
P9 © NEGOVURA/shutterstock.com, © Zern Liew/shutterstock.com, © 2009 Jupiterimages Corporation, © 2008 Jupiterimages Corporation, © Sign N Symbol Production/ shutterstock.com
P10 © omnimoney/shutterstock.com
P16 © iStockphoto/Thinkstock
P18 © 2009 Jupiterimages Corporation
P19 © jehsomwang/shutterstock.com, © TacoLlama/shutterstock.com
P20 © David Spieth/Shutterstock.com
P21 © ColinCramm/shutterstock.com
P22 © Klara Viskova/shutterstock.com, © Clipart.com
P25 © iStockphoto/Seçil Çokan;
P31 © inkspotts/Shutterstock.com, © owatta/ Shutterstock.com, ©2008 Jupiterimages Corporation

British Library Cataloguing in Publication Data
A Catalogue record for this publication is available from the British Library

Contributor: Karina Law
Page design by G Brasnett, Cambridge and Contentra Technologies
Illustrated by Kathy Baxendale, Rachel Annie Bridgen, Andy Tudor and clipart.com, a division of Getty Images
Cover design by Sarah Duxbury and Paul Oates
Cover illustration ©ColinCramm. Shutterstock.com
Project managed by Katie Galloway and Sonia Dawkins

Contents

Words ending in –le

Some words end in –le.

candle   jungle   angle

1 Use the –le words in the box to answer the clues.

> simple   handle   rectangle   bangle   thistle

Another word for bracelet _____

This opens a door _____

A prickly plant _____

The opposite of tricky _____

A shape with four sides _____

2 Draw lines to link the rhyming –le words.

candle   tangle   tumble   trouble   twinkle

angle   sprinkle   handle   double   jumble

3 Write two rhyming words that use each of these –le endings.

–angle _____   _____

–umble _____   _____

Words ending in –el

The –**el** spelling at the end of a word is not as common as –**le**.
–**el** is used after the letters **m, n, r, s, v, w**.

cam**el**

1 Use words from the box to complete the sentences.

> **towel   easel   kestrel   kennel**

Don't forget to take a _____ when you go swimming.

We looked at the artist's picture on his _____.

The dog went to sleep in its _____.

A _____ is a bird of prey.

2 Write a sentence using each of these words.

travel _____

_____

tunnel _____

_____

squirrel _____

_____

Words ending in –al

Lots of adjectives end in –**al**.

The Morris family had a very spec**ial** and magic**al** holiday at Disney World.

1 Add –**al** to these words to make adjectives. Write the adjectives.

electric _____   fiction _____

tropic _____   accident _____

music _____   nation _____

2 Some nouns also end in –**al**.

Write the name of each picture using a word that ends in –**al**.

_____

_____

a ▶ A _____ letter

Words ending in –il

The **–il** spelling at the end of a word is not very common.

lent**il**

1 Solve the clues to complete the crossword puzzle.

fossil	nostril
until	pupil

Down

1. The _____ is the dark spot in the centre of your eye.

2. The _____ is part of the nose. We have two of them and we breathe through them.

Across

3. A _____ is found in rock. It is left over from a plant or animal that lived millions of years ago.

4. "Will you wait for me _____ I get back?"

2 Add **–il** to finish these words and then draw a line to the correct picture.

gerb _____

daffod _____

penc _____

> **What did the cross-eyed teacher say?**
>
> **I can't control my pupils.**

Spelling the 'j' sound with j and g

Listen to the sound of **j** in **j**ar.
The j sound is often spelt with the letter **g** when it comes before **e**, **i** or **y**.

gem

giraffe

gymnast

1 Choose a word from the box that matches each picture. Write the words under the pictures.

| jacket | jelly | juice | jungle | gym | jeans |

  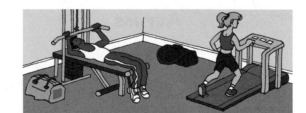 

_____   _____   _____

_____   _____   _____

2 Use a dictionary to find out whether the missing letter is **j** or **g** in these words.

e_____ect   ener_____y   ma_____ic

ad_____ust   sta_____e   en_____oy

8

Spelling the 'j' sound with –dge and –ge

The letter **j** is never used at the end of a word.
At the end of a word, we spell the 'j' sound as:
–**dge** after a short vowel sound   or   –**ge** after all other sounds.

bri**dge**

ca**ge**

1   Find and circle these words that end in –**dge** or –**ge**.

badge
change
fudge
hedge
luggage
village

f	v	i	l	l	a	g	e
q	l	v	f	p	e	b	g
c	g	o	u	j	u	a	h
h	e	m	d	s	e	d	k
a	b	w	g	r	l	g	c
n	y	h	e	d	g	e	s
g	n	l	x	d	m	t	h
e	l	u	g	g	a	g	e

2   Write the words from the word search under the pictures.

_____

_____

_____

_____

_____

_____

The letter c before e, i and y

The letter **c** usually makes an 's' sound when it appears before **e**, **i** and **y**.

certificate

circus

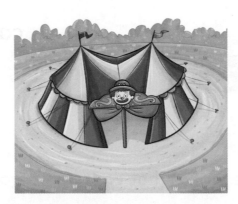

cycle

1 Write each word next to the correct clue.

> iceberg   city   circle   cinema   cereal
> centre   cellar   ceiling   cylinder

A round shape with one side

_____

A very large piece of ice that floats in the sea

_____

A place where people go to watch a film

_____

A room under a house

_____

The middle

_____

A very large town with lots of buildings

_____

Food that we eat with milk for breakfast

_____

A 3D shape with a circle at each end

_____

The part of a room that is above your head

_____

Suffixes –ly and –ful

–**ly** and –**ful** are suffixes.
A **suffix** is added to the end of a word.

love**ly**   play**ful**

> When we add –**ly** to a word that ends
> in **y**, we have to change the **y** to an **i**.
>
> happ**y** + **ly** = happ**ily**

1 Add –**ly** or –**ful** to each of these words.

peace_____   help_____   harm_____

neat_____   doubt_____   lone_____

2 Add –**ly** or –**ful** to these words to make new words. Write the new
words below.

forget quiet silent year slow **hope** quick **mind**

_____   _____

_____   _____

_____   _____

_____   _____

3 Add –**ly** to these words. Make sure you spell the finished words correctly.

tidy + ly = _____   busy + ly = _____

easy + ly = _____   merry + ly = _____

Suffix –ment

–**ment** is a suffix.

A **suffix** is added to the end of a word.

measure**ment**

1 Choose a word from the box that matches each picture. Write the word under the picture it matches.

entertainment   achievement   equipment

_____   _____   _____

2 Tick (✓) the words that can have the suffix –**ment** added to them and cross (✗) the words that cannot. Try saying each word aloud to check if it sounds right.

enjoy ☐   encourage ☐   repay ☐   thank ☐

bear ☐   develop ☐   sore ☐   settle ☐

3 Write a sentence using each of these words.

amazement _____

_____

equipment _____

_____

Suffixes –less and –ness

–**less** and –**ness** are suffixes.
A **suffix** is added to the end of a word.

fear**less**   dark**ness**

When we add a **suffix** to a word ending
in **y** (sounding '**ee**'), we need to change
the **y** to an **i** before adding the suffix.

emp**ty** + **ness** = empt**iness**

1 Add **less** or **ness** to each of these words.

price _____   care _____   harm _____

sad _____   tooth _____   weak _____

2 Complete these word sums. Make sure you spell the finished words
correctly.

tidy + ness = _____   lovely + ness = _____

dizzy + ness = _____   crazy + ness = _____

3 Write as many words as you can that use the suffix –**less**.

_____

_____

_____

Suffixes –tion and –sion

The suffix –**ion** usually has a **t** or **s** in front of it. It changes the meaning of a word and how it is used.

celebra**tion**   deci**sion**

Most words that end with a 'shun' sound have the suffix **tion** or **sion**.

1 Draw lines to link the rhyming –**tion** and –**sion** words.

discussion	potion
lotion	attraction
deletion	invention
collision	percussion
subtraction	completion
attention	division

2 Add **tion** or **sion** to complete these words.

ac_____   occa_____   sta_____

divi_____   direc_____   men_____

frac_____   televi_____   addi_____

3 Write a sentence using as many –**tion** and –**sion** words as possible.

_____

_____

_____

Adding -s, -ed and -ing to verbs

Verbs are action words.

run ⟶ **running**

slip ⟶ **slipped**

If the verb ends in **e**, just add **s**. Drop the **e** when you add **ed** and **ing**.

amuse**s**   amus**ed**   amus**ing**

If the **second to last letter is a single vowel**, usually you just add **s**. Double the last letter before you add **ed** and **ing**.

drag**s**   drag**ged**   drag**ging**

1 Fill the gaps in the table.

Verb	+ s	+ ed	+ ing
cook		cooked	
knock			
hop			hopping
argue	argues		

2 Complete these word sums. Make sure you spell the finished words correctly.

slip + ing = _____   run + s = _____

label + ed = _____   circle + ing = _____

scrub + ed = _____   relax + ing = _____

drop + s = _____   travel + ed = _____

An exception to this rule are the letters **w**, **x** and **y**, which are never doubled. For example: mix ⟶ mixing, mixed.

Adding -y

Adding –**y** to a word changes its meaning.
There are some rules you need to remember when adding –**y**.

Most words	Just add **y**.	dirt + **y** = dirt**y** thirst + **y** = thirst**y**

1 Add –**y** to the words in the box to make new words. Write the new words in the correct places on the weather chart.

rain	wind	storm	cloud	snow

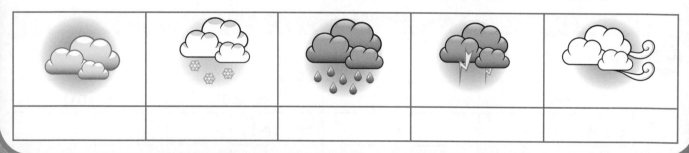

Words that end in e	Usually drop the **e** before adding **y**.	juic**e** + **y** = juic**y** shak**e** + **y** = shak**y**
Words in which the second to last letter is a single vowel	Double the last letter before adding **y**.	spo**t** + **y** = spo**tty** cha**t** + **y** = cha**tty**

2 Complete these word sums. Make sure you spell the finished words correctly.

dust + y = _____   mud + y = _____   taste + y = _____

fun + y = _____   chat + y = _____   giggle + y = _____

Adding –er and –est

Adding –**er** or –**est** to a word changes its meaning.
tall → **taller** → **tallest**
There are some rules you need to remember when adding –**er** or –**est**.

Words that end in e	Just add **r** or **st**.	close + **r** = clos**er** close + **st** = clos**est**
Words that end in y	Change the **y** to an **i** before you add **er** or **est**.	dusty + **er** = dust**ier** dusty + **est** = dust**iest**
Words in which the second to last letter is a single vowel	Double the last letter before you add **er** or **est**.	big + **er** = big**ger** big + **est** = big**gest**

big

bigger

biggest

1 Add –**er** and –**est** to each of these words. Complete the table.

	+ **er**	+ **est**
cold		
hot		
sleepy		

2 Write your own sentence using the words below. The first one has been done for you.

fast, faster, fastest Kirsty is fast, Veejay is faster but Meg is the fastest.

messy, messier, messiest _____

_____

Words ending in –ey

Lots of words end in **–ey**.

don**key**

1 Write a word ending in **–ey** to label each picture.

 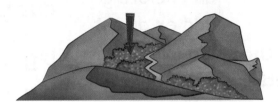 

_____   _____   _____

_____   _____   _____

2 Use a word from the box to complete each sentence.

| valley | joey | chimney | smiley |

A baby kangaroo is called a _____.

I always put a _____ face in my text messages.

An area of low ground between mountains is called a _____.

Smoke from a fireplace escapes through the _____.

Words with 'or' or 'ar' after w

When the 'er' sound follows **w**, it is sometimes spelt **or**.

worm

1 Find and circle these words that begin with **wor**.

w	b	v	w	o	r	l	d
o	u	d	i	s	w	b	g
r	o	g	c	u	o	j	i
s	e	v	w	o	r	k	w
h	w	t	o	o	s	h	o
i	k	h	s	p	t	g	r
p	l	m	d	q	r	t	t
w	n	w	o	r	d	f	h

- **word**
- **work**
- **world**
- **worship**
- **worst**
- **worth**

When the 'or' sound follows **w**, it is sometimes spelt **ar**.

wardrobe

2 Write a sentence using each of these words.

warning _____

_____

warm _____

_____

towards _____

_____

Words ending in –all, –alk and starting with al–

Lots of words end in –**all** or –**alk**.

f**all**

st**alk**

1 Write words rhyming with **all** that begin with letters in the box.

b   c   h   t   w   sm

_____   _____   _____

_____   _____   _____

2 Write three words that end in –**alk**.

t _____   w _____   ch _____

Some words start with **al**–.

Ollie is **al**most as tall as Molly.

Ollie Molly

3 Choose a word beginning with **al**– to complete each sentence.

altogether   always   also

When you cross a road, _____ look both ways.

I love cherries and I _____ like grapes.

We collected over a hundred pounds _____.

Silent 'k' and 'g' in 'kn' and 'gn'

The 'n' sound is sometimes spelt **kn** or **gn** at the beginning of words. Hundreds of years ago people used to sound out the **k** and **g** in these words, but now they are silent.

knee   gnome

1 Circle the silent letters in each sentence.

My dad won the knobbly knees competition.

A mouse gnawed at my gran's knitting.

2 Add the missing silent letter to complete each word. Then write the whole word.

_____nock   _____

_____now   _____

_____nome   _____

_____not   _____

_____naw   _____

_____nickers   _____

_____nit   _____

_____nat   _____

_____nife   _____

_____night   _____

Silent 'w' in words beginning with wr–

The 'r' sound is sometimes spelt **wr** at the beginning of words.

wren

wreck

1 Write a word beginning with **wr**– that rhymes with each word below.

kite → _____

long → _____

tap → _____

twinkle → _____

twist → _____

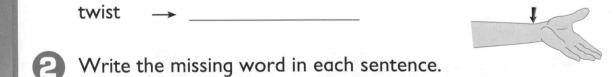

2 Write the missing word in each sentence.

(**wrote**   **write**   **written**)

Yesterday, I _____ a story.

Today, I have _____ a poem.

Tomorrow, I will _____ a song.

Words ending in –y that rhyme with fly

At the end of words, the long 'i' sound is usually spelt with a **y**.

fl**y**

1 Use the letters in the box and the letter **y** to write words that rhyme with **fly**. Cross off each set of letters as you use it.

| cr | sp | dr | tr | repl | sh | fr | sk | wh |

_____   _____   _____

_____   _____   _____

_____   _____   _____

2 Use words from question **1** to complete the sentences.

I wonder _____ the _____ is blue.

I wish you would _____ to _____ to my letter.

"Don't _____!" I said to the unhappy, _____ girl.

3 Which month rhymes with fly? _____

Adding –es to words that end in –y

When we add –**es** to words that end in –**y**, to make them plural, we usually have to change the **y** to **i**.

baby babies

1 Rewrite each word by adding **es**. Remember to change the **y** to **i**.

fly _____   try _____

reply _____   puppy _____

spy _____   story _____

lady _____   berry _____

2 Write the **plural** word under each picture.

| fairy | lorry | pony |

_____   _____   _____

For nouns that end in –**ey** we just add –**s** to make them plural.

3 Write the plural for each of these words.

key _____   monkey _____

trolley _____   jockey _____

donkey _____   journey _____

The letters 'wa' and 'qua'

In some words the letter **a** does not make its usual sound.
It makes a short 'o' sound after the letters **w** and **qu**.

watch

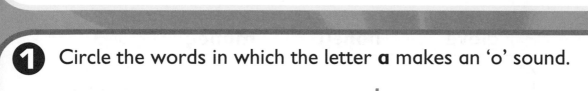

1 Circle the words in which the letter **a** makes an 'o' sound.

wave   wake

swallow   want

wander   squad

quack

quarrel   squawk

squash

2 Write the word next to each picture. Remember to use the letter **a** to make the short 'o' sound.

_____

_____

_____

Words with 'o' as in mother

In some words, the letter **o** does not make its usual sound. It makes a short 'u' sound, as in the word **up**.

monkey

1 Use a word from the box to label each picture.

glove   honey   money

_____   _____   _____

2 Use a word from the box to complete each sentence.

won   other   brother   Monday   nothing   wonderful   love   cover

My _____ is younger than me.

I _____ the egg and spoon race.

I _____ my mum.

We have to go back to school on _____.

I don't like this photo, I prefer the _____ one.

I've eaten everything – there is _____ left on my plate.

Gran put a _____ over the cake to keep the wasps away.

My teacher thinks my spelling is _____!

Apostrophes to show missing letters

We use an **apostrophe** to show where we have put two words together and squeezed one or more letters out! This is called a **contraction**.

she **is** = she's   we **ha**ve = we've

An apostrophe looks like a flying comma.

1 Write the words from the box that these contractions are made from.

> **I will**   should not   **you are**   they have   she will   **we are**

she'll _____   we're _____

they've _____   shouldn't _____

I'll _____   you're _____

2 Complete these word sums to make words with apostrophes. Make sure you spell the finished words correctly.

it + is = _____   they + will = _____

have + not = _____   he + has = _____

I + have = _____   did + not = _____

is + not = _____   he + will = _____

3 Write a sentence using as many different contractions as you can.

_____

_____

_____

The possessive apostrophe: 's

We add **'s** at the end of a singular noun to show that something belongs to that person or thing.

This is Sarim**'s** scarf.

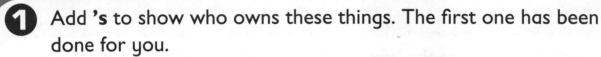

1 Add **'s** to show who owns these things. The first one has been done for you.

This is Emma**'s** ice cream.

These are Ali_'s_ paints.

This is the queen_'s_ crown.

This is Joe_'s_ mum.

This is Sam_'s_ shed.

This is the clown_'s_ wig.

2 Think of suitable words to complete the sentences to show who owns what. Remember to add **'s**.

This is the ___teacher's___ desk.

These are ___dad's___ clothes.

Remind your child that we add just **s** on its own to make a word plural. We should not use an apostrophe to make a noun plural.

Common exception words

Some common words do not follow the usual spelling patterns.

beautiful girl

We need lots of practice to learn how to spell these tricky but useful words.

1 Look at the words in the spelling test.
If they are spelt correctly, give them a tick (✓).
If they are spelt incorrectly, give them a cross (✗).

because

1. becaus ✗

2. child ✓

3. beutiful ✗

4. hour ✓

5. move ✓

6. proove ✗

7. sugar ✓

8. half ✓

9. eye ✓

10. could ✓

11. shood ✗

12. would ✓

13. meny ✗

14. people ✓

15. warter ✗

16. only ✓

2 Now write the words that you have marked with a cross, **correctly**.

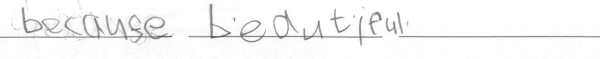

because beautiful

Homophones

Some words sound the same but have different spelling patterns and different meanings. These words are called homophones.

pear  pair

1 Choose the correct word and write it next to the picture.

bear or bare? _____

hair or hare? _____

sun or son? _____

2   two or too? _____

flour or flower? _____

8+6=14   sum or some? _____

night or knight? _____

2 Use some of these homophones to write two sentences. Use a dictionary to check the difference in meaning.

see sea   whole hole   **blue blew**   **here hear**   **one won**

_____

_____

_____

Encourage your child to use a dictionary to check the spellings of homophones and other words. Challenge them to dictionary races with a sibling, or time them using a stopwatch.

Words with 's' as in television

In some words, the letter **s** does not make its usual sound. It sounds like 'zh'.

television

1 Write the correct ending to complete each word. Then write out the full word. Choose from the endings in the box.

> sion　　　　sure　　　　sual

mea_____

deci_____

unu_____

ca_____

plea_____

vi_____

2 Choose from these words to label each picture.

> treasure　　　　explosion

_____　　_____

Answers

Words ending in –le

Page 4

1 bangle, handle, thistle, simple, rectangle

2 candle – handle, tangle – angle, tumble – jumble, trouble – double, twinkle – sprinkle

3 Possible answers include bangle, tangle, mangle
   Possible answers include mumble, bumble, jumble

Words ending in –el

Page 5

1 towel, easel, kennel, kestrel

2 Child's own sentences using the words provided.

Words ending in –al

Page 6

1 electrical, fictional, tropical, accidental, musical, national

2 hospital, pedal, capital

Words ending in –il

Page 7

1 pupil, nostril, fossil, until

2 gerbil, daffodil, pencil

Spelling the 'j' sound with j and g

Page 8

1 juice, gym, jungle, jeans, jacket, jelly

2 eject, energy, magic, adjust, stage, enjoy

Spelling the 'j' sound with -dge and –ge

Page 9

1

f	v	i	l	l	a	g	e
q	l	v	f	p	e	b	g
c	g	o	u	j	u	a	h
h	e	m	d	s	e	d	k
a	b	w	g	r	l	g	c
n	y	h	e	d	g	e	s
g	n	l	x	d	m	t	h
e	l	u	g	g	a	g	e

2 hedge, badge, fudge, change, village, luggage

The letter c before e, i and y

Page 10

1 circle, iceberg, cinema, cellar, centre, city, cereal, cylinder, ceiling

Suffixes –ly and –ful

Page 11

1 peaceful, helpful, harmful, neatly, doubtful, lonely

2 forgetful, quietly, silently, yearly, slowly, hopeful, quickly, mindful

3 tidily, busily, easily, merrily

Suffix –ment

Page 12

1 equipment, achievement, entertainment

2 enjoy ✓, encourage ✓, repay ✓, thank ✗, bear ✗, develop ✓, sore ✗, settle ✓

3 Child's own sentences using the words provided.

Suffixes –less and –ness

Page 13

1 priceless, careless, harmless, sadness, toothless, weakness

2 tidiness, loveliness, dizziness, craziness

3 Possible answers include helpless, hopeless, painless, spotless, useless, loneliness, homeless

Suffixes –tion and –sion

Page 14

1 discussion – percussion, lotion – potion, deletion – completion, collision – division, subtraction – attraction, attention – invention

2 action, occasion, station, division, direction, mention, fraction, television, addition

3 Child's own sentence using as many **tion** and **sion** words as possible.

Adding –s, –ed and –ing to verbs

Page 15

1 cook – cooks – cooked – cooking
   knock – knocks – knocked – knocking
   hop – hops – hopped – hopping
   argue – argues – argued – arguing

2 slipping, runs, labelled, circling, scrubbed, relaxing, drops, travelled